THE
SELF-AWARE
PARENT TWO

23 MORE LESSONS
FOR GROWING WITH
YOUR CHILDREN

CATHY CASSANI ADAMS,
LCSW, PCI CERTIFIED PARENT COACH

ISBN: 1461109876
ISBN-13: 9781461109877
Library of Congress Control Number: 2011906252

Table of Contents

Acknowledgements

Dedicated to Todd, Jacey, Camryn, and Skylar: you inspire me to write, teach, listen, learn, and love.

∾

To my family and friends: I know for sure that life is about relationships, so I am grateful for the life I have with you around me.

To Pagatim.fm, Chicago Parent, Dominican University, and Elmhurst Yoga Shala: thank you for supporting what I have to share.

To my teachers: thank you for guiding me, grounding me, and reminding me why I am here.

To you, the reader: thank you for making yourself a priority. You are a gift to your family and a gift to the world.

It takes courage to grow up and be who you really are. ~ e.e. cummings

Introduction

Camryn, five years old: *"Mom, is anything possible?"*
Me: *"Absolutely."*
Camryn: *"But crayons can't fly."*
Me: *"Why not?"*
Camryn: *"I don't know . . ."*
About ten minutes later . . .
Camryn: *"What if I draw a crayon, and then cut it out, and then hold it in front of the fan. Then it will fly through the air!"*
Me: *"Sounds like crayons can fly."*
Camryn: *"I'm so glad anything is possible."*
Me: *"Me too."*

Children inspire me. They view life with an open mind and creative spirit. They carry a sense of confidence, a belief in who they are and what they can do.

This is how they come into the world, which means at one time, we were all this way. We all believed in ourselves, knew who we were, and allowed our hearts to guide us. But as we grew up, formal education, parenting, and any number of experiences shifted our perspective to the importance of being like everybody else, looking to others for answers, and becoming what other people hoped we would be.

This isn't done maliciously; it's often done with love. Who doesn't want their children to fit in? Who doesn't want their children to be accepted by society? But blending in and being like everyone else can also cause us to lose touch with our true selves—our individuality, our creativity, our personal expression.

Usually, at some point in our lives, we decide it's time to get back in touch with our true selves. We may feel a void, an emptiness or detachment from our everyday lives, even if our lives look pretty good on paper. We want to figure out who we were before we worked so hard to blend in. We want to quiet the running tape of "shoulds" in our head so we can listen to what we really want.

This self-awareness or self-discovery is often perceived negatively, like a mid-life crisis, a luxury, or a selfish act. But in reality, this is an awakening—an amazing realization that we can choose to live a more meaningful life. And this realization is not just a gift to ourselves, it's a gift to others. Realizing who we are and what we have to offer allows us to be truly present for our relationships. The more we know and love ourselves, the more love we can offer others. The process of self-discovery is far from selfish; it's actually a first step toward giving more.

Parenting is our highest calling and our most important work, so it's essential that we take responsibility for who we are and what we do. Our choices not only affect us, they affect the people around us, the most important relationships, the people we love the most. And the heart of life is *relationships*. We tend to think it's about other things—money, power, status, stuff—but real happiness and a full life comes from knowing ourselves, respecting ourselves, and sharing ourselves with others.

Early in my career as a teacher and therapist I had it half right—I was sharing myself with others, listening to others, focusing on other people's issues, but I was unwilling to look at myself. I believed I should already have it all together, and I was willing to be unhappy or pretend in the name of keeping up this façade.

But as the demands and changes of parenthood came into my life, I realized that pretending and being everything to everyone was too tiring. To be a healthy mom, wife, and person and I needed to take care of me.

This meant that I had to be vulnerable—realize my weaknesses and analyze my misperceptions. I had to let go of my need to be right, and I had to ask others for help. I had to realize my worth so I could make myself a priority, and I had to sit in silence so I could hear what was going on inside. And through this often uncomfortable process, I realized I was finding freedom.

Freedom from thinking I need to be perfect, freedom from pretending to be someone I am not, freedom from volunteering for things I didn't want to do or taking jobs that didn't interest me because I thought I "should." Freedom to say, "I don't know," instead of offering an uninformed response, and freedom from pretending to be happy all the time when I, like everybody else, experienced a full range of emotions.

It's now clear to me when I am acting scared, small, or guilty. I notice when I am playing a role or pleasing someone else because I want to be accepted. And if I happen to not notice, I have a husband, friends, and teachers that remind me to take a second look.

There is a voice inside that likes to tell me I am not enough, that I need to do more—keep working, keep making others happy, keep producing, keep pretending, keep tiring yourself out for the sake of others. But there is another voice inside me, a gentler and more trusting voice, that reminds me I am enough as I am.

I am enough even if I don't enjoy playing Barbies or dolls on the floor. I am enough when my kitchen floor is dirty. I am enough when I don't have an answer to your question. I am enough when my children have a tantrum in public. I am enough when I forget an appointment or have to disappoint someone.

I am enough, and so are you. We have our own strengths and weaknesses, we have our own history and current day circumstances, but by nature we are similar because we want the same thing: to feel comfortable in our skin, give and feel love, believe in what we are doing, and feel necessary in this world. And this can't come from outside validation—that's subjective and fleeting. It has to come from inside, from that deep knowing we were born with.

Helping children hold onto this deep knowing is a parenting skill. Allowing our children to tell us who they are rather than telling them who to be is a constant practice, it's not always easy, but it's essential work if we really want them to embrace their own life—the life they came here to live.

The best way to teach this is to role model what it looks like. To fully realize the life you came here to live, and to understand and appreciate who you are so your children can see self-awareness in action. You may need to be vulnerable and open-minded as you try something new; or brave and trusting as you let go of something that isn't working. You may need to admit to past mistakes, feel your emotions, or carve out much needed time for self-care and silence. But these difficult steps are the first steps toward freedom—the freedom to realize how amazing you really are and how much you have to offer.

The essays in this book are reflections on my self-care and my parenting. These are *my* personal experiences, but my hope is that an idea or awareness resonates with you or reminds you of something you already know. This is a parenting book but also a personal growth book—it holds lessons for realizing your full potential so your children are given permission to realize theirs.

And as you realize who your children are, you can let go of the need to always teach and judge and allow them to inspire *you*. Inspire you to think like they do—embrace your emotions, trust your instincts, and be curious just for the sake of being curious. To remind you of what it feels like to trust, to view the world with an open heart and mind, and to know for certain that anything is possible.

Fear as My Friend

I wrote this during the recession and swine flu pandemic, when every television, radio, and newspaper was bracing us for impending doom. The information was everywhere, and I was struggling to stay present; I could feel worry and fear growing.

All media frenzies eventually pass, and with each challenge we can develop a deeper sense that we can make it through difficult times. We can pull from this knowledge the next time a crisis interrupts our lives and make a choice in how we want to deal with it. Do we become anxious, worried and fearful, or do we discover new ways to be aware and calm, to realize that the world does not benefit from our fear, it benefits from our peace.

∽

Right now it feels like old ways are no longer effective—a big shift is taking place. This can be exciting—it's an opportunity for growth and awareness, a chance to make some new life choices. But with growth comes the inevitable growing pains. Our country, our state, and just about every person out there has been feeling the pain. My own family has taken some serious blows—job loss, empty buildings, a house on the market for over a year, dealing with financial loss—not to mention fearing the flu and all of the international happenings. Change can be challenging, and change can evoke fear.

Fear is an old familiar pattern of mine—I have been known to go from 0-60 pretty quickly. In the last few years I have been working hard to create a new relationship with fear, it needed a different role, so I decided that fear and I were better off friends. When fear is my friend it protects me from things or people that aren't good for me, it partners with my intuition to let me know if something is a good or bad choice, and it reminds me if I am not paying enough attention to myself.

If I give my fear too much play, our friendship will inevitably be strained. It morphs into something ugly; it turns into worry, stress, or anxiety—a state of mind created by too much thinking. Fear takes me into the past or it tries to get creative with the future, neither of which I can touch in this moment. Finding balance between friend and foe is my daily work—I am always seeking a comfortable space to sit in.

One thing I do know is that today deserves a lot more love. How are things right now, in this moment? Can I see what is real rather than what is false? Is the sun shining (even if there are clouds, it's still there) and are the leaves beautiful? Do I still have the choice of how to feel every day? Am I going to let the nightly news tell me what to think? I believe that I have the right to decide how to feel.

It's tough out there for a lot of people. No denial here. But as I lie on the couch and watch my girls laugh and jump on their dad, they demonstrate what it means to be on a moment-to-moment happiness mission. They don't care what the stock market looks like and they don't care about the latest governmental debate. They aren't thinking about something they said to someone yesterday and they are not worried about next year. *They are here.* They haven't learned how to live in the past and future yet. I don't want to teach them. I would rather they teach me.

Small decisions help. No television tonight and the newspaper is still on the grass. I chose a good book instead of Newsweek and I deleted all of my e-mails filled with fear and warning. I will stay informed, but I refuse to be inundated; I want to hold onto to some of my own thoughts and create my own expectations.

I am calmed by knowing that the dark brings the light and that challenging times bring awareness and clarity. I can't predict tomorrow, no one can. All I can do is use faith and trust to balance out my fear and focus more attention on my true loves and my daily life. Change is inevitable. And with it comes issues that need to be dealt with. I will put in the time, but I plan to whistle while I work.

Guiding Mistakes

Children tend to carry a great deal of fear about making mistakes, often because they are afraid of disappointing their parents or other authority figures—the people they care for the most.

Parents must teach right from wrong and the rules of society, but it is also a parent's job to teach their children that mistakes happen, and that they are often great learning experiences. Mistakes do not define who we are; they define where we need to go next.

My daughter is in first grade and she is having her first experience with behavior modification. Every student has a clip and inappropriate behavior may necessitate moving the clip to a certain color.

When I ask my daughter about her day she shares a few details and always ends with "I didn't have to move my clip!" At the beginning of the year I found myself saying things like, "Great job!" and "Good for you!" Supportive things that any mother would say.

But now it is the middle of the year and I detect something different in her voice. It sounds a little strained, a little flat, possibly with a tinge of worry, when she says, "I didn't have to move my clip today . . ."

Today I answer her differently. When she tells me that she didn't have to move her clip, I say, "What do you think would happen if you had to move your clip?" She looks at me with anxious surprise—as if I just uncovered a deep dark secret.

"I don't know what would happen," she says with wide eyes.

I see an opportunity, but I hesitate. How do I explain to my first grader that mistakes help us become who we are meant to be?

I think back to when I was sixteen, sitting next to my dad in a courtroom. My crimes were nothing of great consequence (trespassing in a park after it closed, out past curfew), but they were poor choices nevertheless.

I remember feeling awful about being in that courtroom. I was down on myself, thinking how I had disappointed anyone who ever knew me. Wondering who I was and how I got there. These are vital questions for a teenager. This was an important moment in my life.

I remember looking up at my dad, still in his suit because he had to leave work early. I remember seeing a slight smile on his face when he looked at me. He didn't think this was funny, nor was he trying to make me feel better. I just think he understood the significance of the moment. He knew this was a rite of passage—maybe not for every sixteen-year-old, but for me.

He knew that mistakes can be gifts if we view them in present time, without the baggage of fear or worry about what everybody else thinks. His smile gave me hope. It was like he already knew that everything would be just fine. The day in the courtroom didn't need to define who I was; instead, it could help me define who I wanted to be. Mistakes are the teachers that allow us to make informed choices.

I respond to my daughter by saying, "You will learn."

She looks at me with confusion and says, "Learn what?"

I tell her that she will learn what it feels like to make a mistake in school and then she can decide whether or not she wants to do it again.

"What if I make the same mistake again?"

"You will continue to learn," I say.

This is an important connection with my daughter because I know she is uncomfortable with mistakes. I hope to give her some room to breathe—to let her know that choices are a part of life and they can't all be good ones.

My younger daughters may fall somewhere else on the behavior spectrum—I may need to offer balance from the other direction. But this daughter needs to know that there are things to learn outside of the box. I don't want her to look at rules and structure as fear inducing or stifling. I would rather she view them as helpful guides along her journey.

Her life choices have just begun and because I am her parent, her choices will affect me. Some will make me angry, some will make me cry, and some will make me extremely proud.

But no matter how I feel, I hope I can conjure up that slight smile. Not because I think her choices are funny, but because I know she is in the process of finding herself. To let her know that I understand the importance of life experience and I trust that her misjudgments will help her find her real path.

The smile that says: Don't worry, I have faith in you. I know who you are.

The Coins

We live in a society attached to stuff. We desire it, we work for it, and we go into debt for it. Usually because we believe it will make us happy and that things somehow validate us or verify the depth of our relationships.

Mementos from loved ones are beautiful and understandably cherished; they may carry a positive energy or provide memories and comfort. But in the end they are still just things; reminders and symbols of the love that you already carry inside of you.

My youngest daughter needs a backpack for preschool so I find myself searching the basement for a useable hand-me-down. Under a pile of stuff I discover a small pink backpack. My older girls used this one for play more than school, but the size is perfect and the clean up seems minimal.

I unzip the top and am surprised to find a bag of coins. Not just any bag of coins, but the coins my husband's stepfather gave my daughter, Jacey, a month before he passed away.

I have not thought about these coins in a long time. The last time I saw them they were on a shelf in Jacey's room. Several times we explained that they were a gift from Grampa Rich and were very special, but at some point they became toys and ended up in a backpack.

I walk into the next room where Jacey is playing and show her the coins. With a calm but obviously annoyed voice I say, "Don't you understand how special these are? Don't you understand that these are not toys? We might have thrown this backpack away and never seen them again."

I proceed to tell her that I would be putting them away so it never happens again. Noticeably upset, Jacey walks upstairs and into her room.

I remain at the bottom of the stairs and instantly know that I handled the situation very poorly. Using "don't you understand" with a child is ineffective because if you are asking the question, you already know the obvious answer is no. Unsure of what to do next, I start looking through the coins and wondering: What would Rich think about this moment?

Rich never had children of his own and when he married my mother-in-law he embraced her children like they were his. They were young adults when he came into the picture, but he never called them stepchildren; they were his children.

He was all about giving. He gave emotionally and monetarily and all he asked in return was time together as a family. He loved holidays and events where he could grill dinner or take us to his favorite Italian restaurant.

He was a great gift-giver, but he always seemed more invested in the occasion, the opportunity to have family moments. Sometimes I watched him look around the room at the people he loved, seeming so thankful just to be there. Like the rest of the family, I appreciated him and his generous nature. We all loved him very much.

We were devastated when Rich was told that he had pancreatic cancer. He was given a grim prognosis, but somehow he defied the odds and made it to my husband's brother's wedding and our wedding, and he was able to meet Jacey, his first granddaughter, on the day she was born. He was quietly hopeful that we would have a girl.

When Jacey was five months old he came to our house with the bag of coins. He wanted Jacey to have them so she would "never be without." I remember he cried a little. He knew his time was limited and this was a going-away gift.

To this day Jacey beams with pride when she sees a picture of Rich holding her as a baby. Her sisters know who Grampa Rich was and they know his importance in the family, but Jacey never misses an opportunity to say, "Grampa died before you were born, but I knew him and he knew me."

This was most evident the night he passed away. In the middle of the night she woke up crying at the top of her lungs, very uncommon for her. Ten minutes later our phone rang and we were told that Rich had died ten minutes ago. Their connection might have been deeper than we can ever understand.

I put the coins back in the bag and walk upstairs to find Jacey crying softly in her room. I tell her that I am sorry for my strong reaction and I know it must be hard for her to understand why the coins are important to big people. I tell her that playing with the coins and putting them in the backpack was not a bad thing. Grampa Rich would have liked that she was enjoying them.

Together we find a new home for the coins, a place that makes us both comfortable.

The coins are meaningful and they carry significance, but they are not Rich. I don't want any of my children to think mere things carry that much power. I would rather share the coins, the pictures, and the stories.

And I would rather embrace the message that Rich lived: *Life is meant to be enjoyed and it's much more meaningful when you are surrounded by the people you love.*

Release

Children know how to release emotion. Sometimes their bodies and minds cannot tolerate another issue or disappointment, and because they are wise, they "release" to get the feelings out of their system.

This is not always comfortable for parents; it's not easy to sit with a child having an emotional experience. But most of the time children are just trying to communicate overload.

Release is often a step toward finding a healthy balance, and as parents we can offer understanding and support as our children regain their equilibrium.

Camryn is playing with stickers and is noticeably disappointed when one rips. She stares at it for a few seconds and then begins to cry. Not any ordinary cry, but a loud wailing cry. I watch her for a minute or two and decide to pick her up and hug her. Her strong response tells me that she is not just crying—she is releasing.

She sits on my lap and cries loud and hard. I don't speak—I just rub her back as she lets it out. Skylar walks over and rubs her foot, a kind gesture from a two-year-old.

I don't think Camryn is crying because of the ripped sticker–the sticker just pushed her over the edge. She may have had a tough day at school or maybe she didn't sleep great. Maybe she asked for something earlier in the day and nobody heard her or maybe she lost her favorite book.

I have days where one thing after the next goes wrong and the simple act of tripping over a carpet throws me into a tailspin. I know how emotional build-up can result in an out of proportion response.

There are so many emotional experiences in the course of a day. Sometimes we work through them and sometimes we just swallow them. Sometimes we need to release them, and in Camryn's case the ripped sticker was an opportunity to let it all go.

I don't always have the patience to respond to my daughter in this way. At times I am *full* with my own stuff and other times I just need to get her to school or finish checking out at the store.

But right now I have the choice to stop what I am doing and comfort her. I know that it feels good to release emotion when someone is holding you. And I know it feels great to be understood.

Staying present for this type of outburst can be challenging. It is not easy to hear her sob. My discomfort urges me to ignore her behavior or tell her to stop.

But those big cries are begging for attention. And if the crying isn't acknowledged, a tantrum might not be far behind. In either situation she is just asking for validation. Can you allow me to cry instead of trying to fix it? Can you accept me instead of telling me to be different?

A full ten minutes pass before Camryn's cries slow down. I quietly say, "Can I do anything to help you?"

She shakes her head no and rests on me for awhile longer. Eventually she jumps down and picks up the sticker book. She looks at the ripped one with a smile and asks, "Could I have a piece a tape? I gotta get back to fixing this thing."

Just Breathe

Yoga has given me many gifts, but one of the most important is learning how to breathe. Breath work is such a powerful tool to deal with emotions, especially heavy emotions such as anxiety.

The breath is the key to the present moment, the realization that anxious thoughts are creations of the mind, usually fear of the past or future, two things that we cannot touch or control. Letting go of worry is not an easy practice, but breath work is the first step towards realizing that we only have this moment—it's the only place we can truly be.

❧

I woke up at 2:30 last night. Most of the time I fall back asleep pretty quickly—exhaustion can do that to you. But last night my brain decided it was a good time to worry. My thoughts wandered all over the place. From the little things (is the front door locked?) to the big things (is our country really safe?).

Nighttime worry takes on a life of its own. It's grandiose, fear inducing, and stressful.

Eckhart Tolle, author of *The Power of Now*, wrote, "Worry pretends to be necessary but serves no useful purpose." In daylight I believe this, but at night I am harder to convince.

Nighttime worry is like a bad fever dream. You spin your wheels with the belief that you are actually accomplishing something.

It reminds me of the *Seinfeld* episode when Jerry puts pen and paper next to his bed to jot down joke ideas in the middle of the night. When he wakes up in the morning none of it makes sense and it drives him crazy–my point exactly.

Thankfully my wise voice made an appearance and reminded me that I was wasting valuable sleep time. So I focused my attention on the one thing that simultaneously calms the body and mind–breathing. Breath work (pranayama) is one of the many wonderful things that yoga has taught me.

We naturally and spontaneously breathe all the time, but the breath is usually quick and shallow–not very calming to the body. Our breath is connected to our thoughts. When stressed or in pain we often hold our breath or simply forget to breathe, but when we are calm we tend to breathe deeper and slower.

So I work in the reverse–I breathe deep and slow to bring on the calm. It gives my "monkey brain" something to focus on and it allows for a deep state of relaxation.

Breath is also my favorite parenting tool. When my kids are frustrated or fearful I remind them to close their eyes and take a deep breath. When we sit down for dinner we take a deep breath before we eat. When the girls are whining or fighting for my attention I close my eyes and breathe so I don't speak or act impulsively.

Sounds simple, but sometimes simple is all you need. Breathing naturally relaxes the body and brings you back to your right mind.

And last night breathing helped me. Well, first I checked the front door, but *then* breathing relaxed me back to sleep.

The Choice to Shine

I have always been drawn to the world of entertainment. Music, movies, television . . . I am in awe of the bigness and the shininess of it all.

Many of us admire the entertainment industry's shininess, but we are challenged to shine in our own lives. Instead, we are self-critical and devaluing, constantly disrespectful of our gifts and our time.

If you choose to put other's needs before your own, you may make others happy and comfortable, but you probably suffer. If you choose the path of making yourself happy in spite of others, you will be lonely. But if you find that beautiful balance of self-love and self-offering, you find the key to contentment.

∾

I'm a huge movie fan, an entertainment trivia buff, and someone who loves all things Hollywood, so the Academy Awards show is like my Super Bowl (or World Series, or whatever your sport of choice). I'm not interested in the designer gowns or which couples walk the red carpet. I am interested in watching someone's life change in front of my eyes. In a moment an actor goes from one of the many to an Academy Award Winner. Opportunities change, choices grow, and a dream is realized.

I am in awe of these moments because more often than not, these actors have taken a risk to play the part that scored them their Oscar nomination. They moved out of their comfort zone or took a role that nobody thought they could tackle. They listened to their gut or took a leap of faith.

Year after year this has inspired me and served as a reminder. For most of my adult life I have played it safe, stayed within the norm, and looked to others for validation. But in the last couple of years I have made a significant shift. Instead of doing what is expected or assumed, I have made choices outside of my comfort zone. Not just for the sake of being different, but because it's what my heart and soul really wanted to do, and I finally took the time to listen.

Really listening inspired my decision to write, publish a book, have more children, and become a yoga teacher. It also helped me let go of things that didn't serve me, like unfulfilling work or social obligations that I dreaded. Letting go created space for what inspires me on a soul level.

This process of discovery has been the greatest and most difficult work of my life. I have been tested by outside opinion, finances, and finding the right work/life balance. But I have been most challenged by my own insecurity and fear, the part of myself that is uncomfortable with change.

I once heard Oscar Winner Sandra Bullock say that the reason she changed her life, personally and professionally, was because she became "committed to being scared and being braver."

These words resonate so deeply and explain exactly how I feel on a day-to-day basis. Being scared often makes me question my choices and my direction, but I also know that fear is often an indicator that I am doing something worthwhile.

I know that part of my life work is to write and talk about this type of awareness, and even more important, pass this message along to my children. While I am not completely sure how to do this effectively, I do know that listening to myself helps me listen to my children.

Part of my job as parent is to provide structure and safety while teaching my children to live within a society, but the other part is to make sure I hear my children, respect their thoughts, and honor their strengths. To help them trust their inner voice so they live a life that pleases them instead of trying to please everybody else. I know that these concepts cannot be taught with just words. I realize it is something that I need to demonstrate, something I need to live.

And the Academy Awards is one of my favorite reminders of the tremendous possibilities in all of us, and the life-changing opportunities that lie ahead. I may never be an actor, but I know what they mean with they say that all things are possible. I may never be famous, but I understand when they say that a great family and a team of friends helped them get to where they are. I may never meet these people that I have read about my whole life, but I know we are more similar than we are different.

We all want to follow our dreams and live the best possible life. We all want to experience love, discover our life's work, and raise our children with a sense of self and respect for community. We all want to shine. And if we can make the choice to shine, even when outside opinion or fear tells us otherwise, the world becomes a brighter place.

The Process of Pain

This was written after my second miscarriage. I have been through a miscarriage before, but this one was different: less shock, more grief. More understanding of what I needed to do, less understanding of why this was happening again. This was the day after, and all I knew how to do was write.

༄

Life is good. But every once in awhile we have a bad experience, a bad day, or even a bad year. These times can bring confusion, sadness, and heaviness. The lens through which we see the world gets cracked, and nothing looks quite the same.

Right now I have a cracked lens and I am sitting in uncomfortable emotion. I have been here before—pain is the human experience and I have never been, nor do I ever expect to be, immune to it. Historically speaking I have learned a great deal from my pain. It has taught me a lot about who I am and what I really want. Pain can give you the guts to try new things—the what-do-I-have-to-lose mentality. It can also take away your guts, leaving you to struggle with questions and a new reality.

Many things are out of focus, but a few things are quite clear. I am experiencing a renewed and heightened love for who and what surrounds me and I am less worried about the routine items on my list—the shopping and cleaning, the e-mail, the ways I push myself on a daily basis. The ways I mindlessly strive for a perfection that doesn't even exist.

Instead I am hugging my husband, relaxing with my girls, and watching the flowers that are blooming in my front yard. I find myself staring at the most mundane things, squirrels and trees, and wondering about their daily existence. I guess you could say that pain brings you back to earth.

And although I am quite uncomfortable, I am also thankful to be grounded. Pain has slowed me down, reminded me to smile at people, reminded me to be genuine and compassionate. It's an interesting experience to hurt and simultaneously feel significant gratitude about the little things.

It is natural to want to move through pain quickly. We don't have time for it, we don't want to feel it, or it's too scary. But allowing people, things, or activities to simply take away the pain can be a real disservice to the process. If pain is left unresolved it can lead to false thinking or fear. It can shape the way you choose to live the rest of your life. It can leave you stuck instead of free.

I am still in the middle of my hurt so I don't have hindsight for what it all means, but I do feel more tapped into the reality of life. The reality that things don't always go the way I think they should and the reality that I don't have complete control. It's a great relief to know that I can't control all things, and at the same time it's very unsettling.

To protect ourselves from pain we may decide to stay safe by *attempting* to control every aspect of our lives—our activities, our relationships, our children, our work. We may decide to take the mainstream path rather than the road less traveled because it's perceived as a safer route. But following the masses or living someone else's dream does not ensure safety; it can actually be more risky because you miss out on your own life adventure and the world misses out on your gifts.

Feeling safe is possible if we can develop a deep sense of trust. Trust in the process or a trust in something greater than us. Or a trust in ourselves to surrender to the experience of life, which by definition includes pain. These are our opportunities to become stronger and more aware human beings.

The Continuous Climb

I was at another crossroads in life, another decision that needed to be made. I was frustrated, even angry that I was faced with another soul-searching decision. Hadn't I done this already? Haven't I worked hard enough?

But I laugh even as I type those words, because I know what life is, and it is indeed a constant string of choices. And because I choose to be aware and responsible for my choices, I feel the emotion of each decision.

And sometimes I fear what lies ahead, but I also believe that the unknown offers even greater opportunities than what we can even imagine. I trust that as I continue to climb, I will develop a deep trust of each hill and valley, and that each experience is simply a step closer to the person I came here to be.

❦

We are driving through hilly Galena, Illinois, enjoying a family weekend when Jacey points out a long steep road straight ahead. I tell her that her great grandparents, grandma, and great aunt used to live up that road and that we will drive by their old house once we get to the top.

I hear a cry from the back of the car. I turn around and find Camryn shaking her head. She says, "I don't want to go up that hill!" When I ask why she says, "It's too big, it's too scary!"

I quickly climb to the backseat so I can sit by her and nod to my husband to keep driving. I hug her as we begin to ascend the hill. I tell her that I hear her and that I will stay right next to her as she cries and holds on tight.

Right before we hit the top she lets out a scream, but it quickly turns to silence as she catches a view of the other side. In front of her are trees, houses, flowers, and a park. Her only word is, "Oh."

She looks down and then looks at me with a half smile. She seems embarrassed, but I don't feel judgment and I don't believe that her feelings were wrong or silly. I don't want her to feel shame or guilt for feeling her fear.

Climbing that steep hill was like venturing into the unknown and her fear was valid and real. I say, "Do you understand that your mind told you the hill was scary because it was big and you couldn't see what was on the other side? Feeling scared is normal, but sometimes we need to climb the hill to get to where we need to go."

She nods, and like a kid that just rode her first rollercoaster, she says, "Okay . . . let's do it again!"

Driving up the hill while holding Camryn was like the first time I walked her into preschool, the first time I helped her into a big girl swing, and the first time I carried her into a pool. They are new experiences and understandably scary, but they are life steps that need to be taken.

Before that hill came into view I had been sitting in the front seat mulling over some of my own thoughts and fears, going through potential outcomes and worst-case scenarios. My daughter's cry from the backseat was similar to my own thoughts: I'm scared, I'm stuck, I don't know what comes next. It was an important moment, a teaching for her, a realization for me.

Driving up that hill was Camryn's small step toward embracing the unknown, and for me it was a reminder of what I have already experienced and what comes next. Do I dig in my heels and refuse to climb the next hill, or do I let go and roll with it? Of course the unknown can lead to things I don't want to see or experience, but sometimes it's a place filled with trees, flowers, parks, and a new level of self-understanding.

As I move back to my front seat I am barraged by a series of questions and comments from Camryn—this new experience has left her exhilarated, full of energy, full of life. I smile at her and silently thank her for reminding me about my own journey, that the hills can be threatening, but what waits on the other side can be beautiful.

Five Children

This was written six months after my miscarriage. This was one of two miscarriages in my life — the first was before I had my daughter Skylar.

Through this experience I found no definitive answers, but I did find acceptance.

⁓

Months ago I had a miscarriage. My second miscarriage. Like last time, at eleven weeks. Like last time, it was devastating, overwhelming, and difficult to bear. But it was also different than last time. Very different. Instead of my inner voice telling me to heal so I could do it again, it said heal so I could move forward. An uncomfortable thing to hear, it almost felt irrational. *You mean that's it? That's what the last year and a half was for? To get pregnant and have a miscarriage?*

But the voice was clear. I half listened, assuming that at some point it would say something different, that the fear and the grief were hiding my true feelings. But time moved on, and my husband and I could both feel that it was different. And both of our lives started swirling and changing, our relationship becoming front and center again, realizing that we have reached a new stage of parenting. No more high chairs, no more nursing, no more pacifiers.

And I had realizations about myself, who I am, and what I intend to do. The last eighteen months I prepared for a new baby, and now that was not going to be. So different doors were opening, I felt myself growing, literally propelling forward into a new chapter of my life. But did it need to happen this way?

The reality is that I had a child—only for eleven weeks, but a child was here. I was pregnant and then I wasn't, and in that time I learned a great deal. About my ability to trust myself, the strength of my inner guidance, information about who I am and where I feel guided to go.

This pregnancy, this child, allowed another layer of myself to be realized and revealed. And though there may be many other reasons for the child's short time here—things I am not meant to understand—for me it was a heart-breaking and soul-opening experience.

Grief came and I sat in it for months. And then I sat in the guilt of not wanting to be pregnant again. And at some point guilt dissipated, and I realized that a child had come, but was no longer here. That his/her time was short, but important. And that it was indeed different than last time, and that it is okay for it to be different.

Things have changed and I am different. I wouldn't have predicted or wished for this way to discover me, but I will accept it. I don't know if I could have seen it or accepted it any other way.

And my story is not everybody's story. And I don't talk about it much because there are too many layers and no simple answers. But I do know that my life story is forever changed, and when people ask me how many children I have I will say three, but my heart will always say five.

Five children who have guided me and helped me figure out who I am. For my sake and for theirs. Some of my children will offer me lifelong lessons, and some of my children offered me a lesson in time. And I am eternally grateful to all of them, my children—my true loves.

The Girlfriend Trip

Girlfriend trips are essential outings in my life — the more the better. Getting lost in the minutia of the day is so easy; it's often difficult to remember who we are. But friends can always bring us back. They call us by our real name or nickname, call us out on our stuff, remind us how to laugh, and bring us back to earth. And this essay is a tribute to the beautiful women in my life, the ones that remind me of who I am.

The girlfriend trip is one of my favorite weekends of the year. It can be a challenge to plan and not everyone can make it every year, but for as long as I can remember it has been a priority.

Some of us have made the trip while nursing an infant and some of us leave a ridiculous pile of work at the office. It's not easy to carve out time and it can be a challenge to say good bye to the family, but ten minutes out the driveway I always remember why I need to go.

For a weekend the two names I love, Mama and Sweetie, are replaced with Cathy or Cassani (what most of my friends from college call me). Two names that help me reclaim a part of myself—before the career, before the family, before the busy life.

The weekend begins with a three-hour drive with Lara. We catch up on all things important and I find myself shifting into "college language" (a little slang, a little cursing). At one point I look at Lara and laughingly apologize for swearing so much. She looks at me confused and says, "I didn't even notice." We so quickly drop our careful mom language and fall back to the way we have always been.

We connect with the rest of the group, relax with a glass of wine, and appreciatively acknowledge the lack of connection to time. A conversation that started at 7:00 p.m. can last until 2:00 in the morning, and our days are not scheduled. If we feel like doing something we do it, but we don't burden our time with expectation. The only burden in the weekend is getting to a spa appointment on time or making sure we make a dinner reservation.

This group knows how to tell stories and laugh, and we make fun of each other for the stupid things we did in our twenties (and thirties). We talk about our present day experiences, and though most stories have happy endings, we have our share of tears, too. It's always a great release, a safe place to share what you are really feeling with people who have loved you your whole adult life.

The highlight of our weekend is the dance party—a girl's weekend staple. In the early days it happened twice a weekend, but as we get older we can only depend on one big night.

Dance party is always my favorite part of the weekend because it's all about letting go. We usually end up with sore muscles, a broken speaker, and sometimes bruises and cuts from attempting dance moves like the worm, or a handstand into the worm.

We listen to old music and my hipper friends introduce me to more current songs. For a night my concerns and agendas are replaced by loud music and dancing, an exercise I have appreciated my whole life, even when I was a little girl listening to the radio.

When Sunday comes we are ready to return to our lives, but I always go back feeling a little different. A little more full and definitely more content. Reconnecting with Cathy Cassani helps me return to Mama and Sweetie with renewed energy—they come together in harmony and I feel more whole.

As I put my daughters to bed on Sunday night I share the details from my weekend—the long nights of talking and dancing, the shopping, the pedicure, the eating out at restaurants, and the visit to the local chocolate store that results in me eating chocolate all weekend. My oldest daughter stares at me with envy and says, "Can I do all that when I'm in my thirties?"

I smile and nod, tuck them in, and make a silent wish of love for all of my daughters. A love of self so they make themselves a priority, companion love like the connection I have with their dad, and the special love of lifetime girlfriends. Friends that keep you grounded and stand by you as you rediscover yourself—on the dance floor, or in life. Friends that hold the memories and continually remind you of who you are.

I love you girls . . .

Feeding Ourselves, Feeding Our Children

Food. It's wrapped up in memories, traditions, emotion, and guilt. It's hard to see clearly when we are feeding ourselves, and this inevitably spills over into our parenting.

It's not just about feeding our kids today. It's about teaching them how to eat for a lifetime. But to do that, we need to figure it out for ourselves.

∽

Oh, food . . . I have learned so much about you in the last couple of years. I have been riveted by the documentary *Food, Inc.*, I have been educated by Michael Pollen's books *The Omnivore's Dilemma* and *Food Rules*, and also Kathy Freston's *Quantum Wellness*. And our whole family fell in love with Jamie Oliver's quest to bring healthy food to schools.

Jamie and the others are getting the nation's attention because they have a big message to share: The food we eat is harming us and it's harming our children. It's hard to hear, but it's time that we hear it.

Honestly, the food topic is so vast I don't even know where to begin. There are so many issues when it comes to what we eat, from government subsidies to family traditions; it's a tough subject to wrap up neatly. And even I struggle while writing this because I know there is a lot of guilt around food, a lot of blame, and a lot baggage that we carry.

But guilt is time consuming, not helpful, and it's a literal waste of energy—why focus on what happened yesterday when you have today and the rest of your life to make changes? Instead, let's move forward with food rather than staying stuck, and let's be honest about why feeding ourselves and our children is so challenging.

Our society tends to view food only from a place of weight loss and body image, and that makes food an obstacle to overcome instead of something to appreciate and enjoy. Children need information so they can use food in a healthy way, not in a way that makes them feel bad about themselves. Eating is often used as an opportunity to demonstrate control or more often lack of control. That process has burden and guilt written all over it.

We need to teach our children to eat from a place of balance and connection to their bodies, so they realize what food can do for their body, how eating well can give them energy, and how eating poorly can diminish their energy. We need to help our children create a positive relationship with food—a relationship that will last the rest of their lives.

Just for the record, I am not a doctor, I am not a health food freak, and I don't believe in diets. I definitely enjoy my occasional order of French fries and chocolate cake, but I also attempt to be thoughtful about my daily choices. I don't restrict or count calories; I just try to eat real food. Food that's not processed (or at least not processed too much). Food that my body can use and food that tastes good.

I am in no way a perfect eater, nor do I try to be. But I have found that if I balance the really good stuff with a few splurges here and there, I feel really good most of the time.

I want my children to view food in a balanced way, too. Yes, they have an occasional hot dog and French fries, they love birthday cake, and at least once a week they get a sucker from my next door neighbor. But instead of telling them how bad a food is or how certain foods will "make them fat" (guilt, guilt, guilt), I want them to notice how they feel.

They are usually sugar-buzzed and then crash after a birthday party, if they eat too many pieces of pizza they end up lying down with a stomachache, and they tend to feel funky after eating a tri-colored fruit roll up. I gently help them realize (again, no guilt trips) that their body does not know what to do with that unhealthy food and that it can cause them to feel yucky.

If I really have their attention I shift my focus to how "real food" (instead of "healthy food" . . . healthy food tends to sound like a carrot stick) helps their brain do homework, run faster in soccer, and it allows their body to sleep well at night. These are the messages I want them to integrate.

As their mom my job is to make good foods accessible. Unfortunately I do not find the kitchen relaxing nor do I take pleasure in cooking a meal. But, I am committed to buying and preparing healthy foods in my house. I am willing to pay a little more for organic fruit and vegetables and I am willing to cut it up and have it ready to eat when my kids are hungry.

Perfection doesn't exist in this process—I just want my children to realize that food is an ally and it's meant to be enjoyable and even medicinal. The food we eat is our first line of defense in being healthy people, emotionally and physically.

This is not easy, I have a daughter who won't eat much, a daughter who will try anything, and one that falls somewhere in the middle. Trying to change everything overnight is not realistic and it can lead to feelings of failure. Our first big choice a few years ago was having organic milk delivered to the house. Then after some time we made another little change, and then another, and so on.

Our newest change is introducing a "vegetable of the week" at family dinner. We cook the vegetable (olive oil and salt do wonders) and also try it raw. We talk about how the vegetable can help our body and mind. By the way, did you know that asparagus can detoxify the system, protect against cancer, reduce pain and inflammation, reduce the risk of heart disease, and it has anti-aging properties?

While I am committed to the health lessons, I am not committed to becoming fanatical. We still have pizza and ice cream every Friday night because it's our family tradition, and because it makes having dessert a once-a-week special occasion.

Above all I am most committed to viewing food in a positive way. I don't want my girls to view food from a place of lack or as something forced on them (I can't have this, I have to have that). I am searching for that place in the middle—a place where they can enjoy what food has to offer while being educated about its effect on the body. I want them to eat for pleasure, but not use food to fill a need for pleasure.

Am I asking too much? Maybe, but I have no immediate goal or milestone that I need to reach. This is a work in progress, a re-shaping of old patterns, and a lifelong educational process—for me, my children, and for the entire nation.

Practicing Mudita

I can easily go down the road of thinking that life isn't fair or that there isn't enough to go around. I don't always get what I want and things don't always turn out the way I planned. At times I feel envy, but I know this is a normal emotion and it doesn't warrant guilt; it just necessitates my awareness.

To come back to the understanding that we all have beauty in our lives and we all have suffering. And to believe that the more love in the world, the better it is for all of us.

❦

Last night I ran across an article in *Yoga Journal* about the practice of *mudita*. It's a Sanskrit word that means "to take active delight in others good fortune or deeds."

Oh, how I needed this article . . . we have been trying to sell our house for, well, let's just say a long time now, and I continue to hear stories about the friend that sold his house in forty-eight hours or the relative that sold her house quickly and for above market value. My response to these stories is usually *grrrrr* . . .

This is my emotional response, fueled by envy and frustration because I am bumming that I am not having the same experience. This is normal, just like feeling *grrrrr* when your friend goes on a long kid-free vacation is normal, or when your best friend's baby sleeps through the night immediately, or when you hear that all your sister's children are academically gifted, or when your neighbor was just offered the part-time job of her dreams.

But it's simply an initial response, and it doesn't need to be self-defining. Just acknowledge the negative feeling because denying it can be more painful than the feeling itself. Having an initial negative response does not necessitate loads of inner criticism (I'm a bad friend, I shouldn't feel this way); it's actually a good reminder and an opportunity for deeper awareness.

It's an opportunity to look more closely at your own joy, to have gratitude for your own life, loves, and experiences. To appreciate *what is* and focus on what is working for you right now, in this moment. Maybe it's a difficult time and you can only find a few things…that's okay, focus on the few things. Finding personal joy is a grounding and mindful experience and it's the first step towards sharing the joy of others.

For me this is actually a selfish act because it feels so much better to be happy for the friend with great news or the neighbor that sold the house quickly. Feeling frustrated or deciding that it isn't fair is just a great big drag. I end up carrying around my own frustration and the frustration that someone else is happy. Not a very healthy or productive use of my time.

Of course it sometimes seems like good things happen to certain people all the time, but take it from a therapist that has worked with a lot of different families, everyone has challenges, no matter who they are. There is no need to compare experiences, pain is pain, and challenges are challenges. We are all living the balance of light and dark, between good times and not-so-good times.

There are people with seemingly endless challenges that choose to focus energy on appreciating their blessings, and there are people who seem blessed beyond measure who choose to focus on their difficulties. We all have a choice on where we want to focus our attention, and practicing *mudita* is an opportunity to focus on the light.

And within that light we can realize that good fortune is limitless. The universe is not a pie with only a certain number of pieces to hand out, it's limitless, and within it is a limitless supply of good fortune. This means that every one of us has the potential for greatness. Or maybe we can grasp that everything is already great and that our real work is just realizing it.

Bottom line is that when a friend sells her house it doesn't mean that I won't. It actually has the opposite effect—it makes it even more possible. Each positive experience spreads more positive energy, and every person that sells a house benefits the community, the economy, and the greater good, which of course benefits me. We are all undeniably connected and we all reap the rewards of each other's joy.

Yes, it's a little idealistic, but I am not completely off my rocker. I still live in this world and I know it's not easy to see things this way. That's why *mudita* is described as a practice. It's the revelation that there is another way, a way to transcend a negative response and find the divine good in it all.

It's the realization that we all benefit from each other's happiness, and that it's about time we join in on the celebration.

The F Word

I am in a new phase of parenting. No longer the mother of toddlers, I am now the mother of three little girls, all of them having their own experiences and relationships outside of our four walls.

I can no longer witness all of their experiences, so I have to keep them safe in a different way. I make myself open and available for honest communication, listen without judgment, and allow them to grow up and experience the world — even when it's hard to hear.

⁂

My daughter walks in and says, "I know what the F word is." Okay, so here we are. She is going into second grade, I knew this was inevitable, but it still feels soon. I ask her what it is and she is correct; she knows the F word.

I ask her where she heard it and she says that it's written on the slide at the park. I guess this is the only downside to being able to read.

I ask her if she has any questions about the F word and she says she wants to know why she can't say it. I explain to her that it's an adult word, but kids like to use it, usually because it makes them feel older.

I tell her that as she gets older she is going to hear this word and other adult words, but that doesn't mean that they are appropriate words to use.

I tell her that there are plenty of words out there to express herself and she doesn't have to use words that can hurt or offend people.

I tell her that if she ever has a question about a word to feel free to talk to me about it. I tell her that as she gets older she will hear more things that might be confusing and part of my job is to make them not so confusing.

She nods and thinks for a few minutes. "I know the S word, too."

Okay, I say, tell me the S word.

Quietly she whispers in my ear, "It's *stupid.*"

I breathe a sigh of relief. I know things are coming and I'm getting ready, but it's nice to know that she can be seven a little while longer.

Calm Creates Calm

When things in my home are feeling out of control, I can naturally become a part of the negative spiral. But if I bring anger to anger or anxiety to anxiety, it only heightens an already overwhelming situation.

If we can practice bringing something different, something lighter like love or calm, we may discover that we can shift the energy of an entire room. I think of it as meditation in motion, or a way to practice yoga off the mat.

~

My husband is traveling, it's 7:00 p.m., and I'm tired. My girls want to go back to the park; they are full of energy and questions. Did I mention I'm tired?

I take responsibility and share how I feel. "Girls, I am tired, and I don't have the energy to go to the park. Instead, we are going to have quiet time at home while I clean the kitchen."

Disagreement all around, comments about how it's summer, it's beautiful outside, and how they want to catch fireflies . . .

I take a deep breath and slow down even more. Slowly and softly I explain that tonight we are staying inside. I allow them to share their frustration; I don't talk, I just listen intently and nod. I slow down even more, keep breathing, keep it together . . .

Time passes and I realize I haven't talked in awhile. I look around the room and the girls are all doing different things—one is cutting paper, one is looking at a book, one is using watercolors. I don't know when they dispersed and got busy doing their own thing, but I do know it feels calm in here, it's quiet, it's relaxed.

I think about Thich Nhat Hanh, a Buddhist monk who shares his message of peace around the world. I have heard that when he walks on stage to present, his peaceful energy brings a sense of calm to the entire room; everyone quiets down and feels his presence.

I don't claim to have the power of a Buddhist monk, but I do believe my girls respond to the energy I carry. Anxiety is contagious (if you have been with someone who is anxious, you know what I mean) and calm can be contagious, too.

So instead of telling my girls to calm down, I can calm down first. Instead of using words, I can use breathing.

Maybe to teach the behavior I need to role model the behavior.

Will this work every time? I don't know.

But it worked today.

Boy Friends

I have always loved the color pink, skirts, dancing, and many other typical female enjoyments. But I also appreciate sports, I wear baseball hats, and I laugh at crass comedy. These typically masculine attributes are important parts of me, too.

We are all onions, blessed with many layers, and life is so much more fun when we are given the freedom to explore all parts of ourselves. Having male friendships gave me the freedom to see beyond my gender-specific role, and it helped me develop a more balanced and positive relationship with the opposite sex.

❦

My girls love playing with the boys on the block. They love their girl-friends, too, but this summer they are developing relationships with the boys.

Together they play basketball in the driveway, they practice karate (they don't know what karate is, but they practice it), they pick up bugs, dig in the dirt, and make up games about woodchips.

I appreciate what I see because I grew up with some great guys, too; guys that I met very early in my life, guys that remained friends through high school and beyond.

I can't say enough about the girlfriends I have had over the years, but my opposite sex friendships have been pretty special, too. They offered me a world of new experiences, a different perspective on how to see myself, how to be more of myself.

I never considered myself "boy crazy"; I just enjoyed the company of boys. My guy friends were funny and uninhibited and they taught me about music, sports, and swear words. And they carried themselves differently, not better or worse than my girlfriends, just differently.

I don't have any brothers so these guys were my teachers. They let me wear their wrestling shoes and their football jerseys. They encouraged me to ride my bike without holding onto my handlebars and they confided in me about things they didn't want to tell their friends.

In seventh grade Jacob and Scott taught me how to spit through my teeth at Sweet Park (gross, I know, but so cool back then . . . I can still do it by the way).

My friend Jerry always knew how to make me laugh when I was struggling, and he liked to make fun of my big eighties hair (he still does). And my friend Brian taught me how to handle, and even throw back, sarcastic comments. He was, and still is, a pro.

Sometimes Jim and Randy would walk me home from school and teach me the words to Van Halen's "Ice Cream Man," and Led Zeppelin's "Thank You" reminds me of Joe (as does Aldo Nova's "Fantasy," a song that will follow him around forever). When I hear Billy Idol I think of Richie and Elvis will always remind me of Justin.

The guys had their own lingo, great words that were easy to pick up. Everything from "pulling ahead" (meaning you made a fool of yourself) to "sick one" (similar description) to "skirdoo!" (very loosely translated as, "all right!" I already know that I will be made fun of for this translation). And the term of endearment "pretty," which my best friend Monisha and I still call each other.

Along the way some of us dated and had more serious relationships, but at the root of it all there was friendship, which made it easier to get back to where we started.

The relationships were not always easy, they could be messy and they required some work, but I am so thankful for the experiences because they were a part of my base, part of the reason my life unfolded as it did.

I left for college with an ability to relate to men and women confidently, to view guys as friends and not just romantic prospects. My first response to a guy was never changing or flirting, it was more honest than that, much more of a peer relationship.

I was even drawn to my husband because of his love of sports, his humor, his appreciation of great music, and because he embodied what it meant to be a good friend. He reminded me of my guys, and I felt right at home.

So this summer I enjoy watching my girls play "sticks" and kick every ball imaginable as their fancy dresses, princess toys, and dolls go untouched. It's fun to watch their awareness and self-concept shift as they investigate different parts of their personalities.

And it's a pleasure to see their definition of "friend" expand, because I know from experience that this will make an impact on, and greatly enhance, their lives.

Be Here Now — What Does This Really Mean?

For a long time I believed that true mindfulness was something I needed to reach, a way to feel consistently connected to the moment. I believed that getting lost in thought or feeling anything other than joy could be deemed unacceptable or a failure.

But over time I learned that we will always have thoughts, and we will always experience the full range of emotions. Mindfulness is about accepting this and being fully conscious of these truths, while simultaneously realizing that a deeper awareness exists inside of each of us, a place that can remain calm and still no matter what the brain thinks or no matter what emotions arise.

∽

After a presentation the other day, a parent approached me and mentioned that she feels guilty about not being fully present or mindful when she is with her children. Although I completely understand her feelings, I also know that guilt is a waste of valuable energy and it's actually a *disservice* to the present moment.

Being present means that instead of being focused on what happened yesterday or what could happen tomorrow, you are simply here, now. It's about getting off autopilot and becoming aware of the automatic actions and reactions you are used to, and finding a place of clarity and calm. The present moment offers peace.

Being present or mindful is not a place that you can remain continuously. It's more of a moment, a glimpse, a feeling, or a deep awareness.

To suspend these moments or feel them more frequently takes practice; mindfulness is a muscle that needs to be worked. The good news is that many different paths lead to the present moment: yoga, prayer, meditation, deep breathing, writing, singing, dancing, playing with your children . . . the list goes on and on.

You don't have to wait to practice mindfulness, you can start this minute. Take a deep breath and feel what is going on in your body.

Some people think that to be mindful you need to turn off your thoughts or silence your brain, but in reality your brain is always working and thinking (some refer to this as "monkey brain").

Instead, think about quieting the parts of the brain that are stuck in the past and future (regret, worry, fear) and turn up and tune into the part that is here now (acceptance, love, appreciation). Be a witness to the endless chatter in your brain (your brain is a processing machine, it can think about things without your consent).

The part of you that notices this, that realizes your brain is talking and thinking without you, is who you really are. Notice you more often. Practice finding you whenever you can.

For example, if you are walking, notice that you are walking. Notice your legs and feel the ground. Look up and feel the sun. If you are eating, take slow mindful bites. Really taste what you are eating. If you are playing with your children, look them in the eyes and listen to them. Focus on what they look like in that moment and how they make you feel.

And if all else fails, just close your eyes and take a good, deep breath. Breathing, something we take for granted, is easy access to the present moment. It brings us back to our bodies, back to our awareness.

I call these moments "taking it in". They are excellent ways to slow down and appreciate *what is*. Experiencing these moments can reduce stress, keep your body working properly, and create more happiness. Do I need to say more?

But please let go of feeling bad about not being constantly present (none of us are!). Mindfulness is simple in concept, but it's a practice and it's not always easy.

View being present as an opportunity rather than a destination, or think of it as a relaxing respite from the continuous processing of your brain. And know that it's always available to you—guilt-free.

Emotional and Physical

The mind and body are entwined, one constantly affecting the other. How we think plays a role in how we feel, and this awareness can help us play a role in our own emotional and physical health.

As a parent I want to teach my children to see the connection, to help them realize that both need to be attended to, and that there are many different paths to healing.

∾

Last Thursday night at 12:30 a.m., my daughter showed up in our bed. She complained of a stomachache, but had difficulty describing it.

"Do you feel like you're going to throw up? Do you need to go to the bathroom? Is it actual pain?"

All questions were answered with, "I don't know."

Neither of us slept much that night, and the next day she was tired with no appetite. She took a bath, we put oils and warm washcloths on her stomach, and she rested. She definitely had physical symptoms, but I wondered if the looming first day of school might be the reason for her discomfort.

In our house we talk a lot about how the mind can affect the body. She has heard that her body responds to the way she thinks, feels, and acts.

But I know from experience that when you are in distress, it's harder to embrace this concept. So instead of lecturing her about the interrelationship between physical and mental health, I just spent time with her so we could talk.

We talked about music and movies, and we talked about school, specifically my grade school experiences. I told her about all of my teachers and how I was always nervous at the beginning of the school year. She listened intently, asked questions, and then took a long nap.

The next day was better, but she still seemed heavy and tired. We continued our talks and I mentioned that I was starting my new job next week, a teaching job at a university. I told her that I felt ready and excited, but also nervous and unsure.

She asked how I make myself feel better, so I told her that I talk about it. Instead of keeping my fears in my mind where they can grow and become scary, I talk about them and even ask her dad (or others) for help if I need it.

That night when I was tucking her in, I could feel her struggle and discomfort, and right before I turned off the light she sat up and said, "I'm feeling nervous and I am going to miss summer and I don't want to be away from home every day for six hours!"

It all came out really fast, she was breathing heavy, and she stared at me, unsure of what just happened. I nodded and said, "That makes sense to me, and it's completely normal."

I didn't try to talk her out of her feelings, and I didn't list all the things she had to look forward to. I just listened, nodded, and let her know that her feelings were okay and understandable. We talked about how great the summer had been and how great it was to wake up late and hang out at the pool.

We talked about second grade, her teacher, and the friends in her class. And when I asked what I could do to help, she already had a plan—she wanted to wear my necklace to school so she could feel closer to home.

I was confident that she would feel a lot better in the morning, but I also realized that her body really had been sick. Maybe it was a stomach bug, or maybe it was entirely mental, but either way it had become physical, and she needed to be taken care of on that level.

To tell her she was silly, wrong, or that it was all in her head would have been disrespectful to her experience. I want her to trust her body and be attuned to its messages, and just as important, I want her to trust me.

So it felt right to walk both paths—soothe the physical and discuss the emotional, with the hope that one, or maybe both, would offer some relief.

And thankfully, she was in good shape yesterday, raring and ready to go for her first day of second grade. Her eyes were bright, she was all smiles, and her outfit choice was based on two things: it was super comfortable, and it really showed off my necklace.

Revel in the Frenzy

Chaos is not my intention, but it is often what I create. I attempt to fill up every moment of the day, staying busy, overloading, because if a moment is free, I might feel uncomfortable, as if downtime equals laziness.

But I know not having downtime is a disservice to myself and my family. We all need time to think, play, read, relax or, simply space out. In these moments clarity has an opportunity to shine through. These are the moments when we fully experience connection. These are the moments that we are always waiting for.

I have an opportunity to relax at 6:00 p.m. This is unheard of; it's usually much later before I get a chance to sit down, so I instantly feel excitement for this gift of time. But quickly my feelings of joy begin to morph into guilt. As if I don't deserve this time, as if I should be doing something more productive with it.

This gift of time quickly becomes a gaping hole that needs to be plugged. I long for peace and time to appreciate the moments, but as much as I hate to admit it, I also revel in the frenzy.

This is not an easy admission. I practice meditation and yoga every day and I teach others to slow down and enjoy their lives. I fully believe in what I teach, but at times I am challenged to put it into practice.

If I revel in the frenzy I don't have to appreciate what is real. The busier I am the more excuses I have to not pay attention to myself, to say no to new opportunities, and to demonstrate how much I extend myself and how hard I am working.

It's like a big convincing show. Don't you see my frenzy? Don't you understand that I don't have time for that? Don't you see that people are counting on me? But as much as my busy mind would choose to disagree, I know in my heart that I always have a choice. I don't have to live this way.

But being frenzied is a built-in excuse to live on the surface. On the surface I don't have to feel my feelings or deal with difficult matters that need to be addressed, and I don't have to take care of myself. It's a draining and inauthentic way to live, but the frenzy is a great convincer.

The best part is that I can easily proceed this way because it's socially acceptable to be frenzied. In fact, it's encouraged. Get a lot done in very little time is our motto. It's a great show, but like all great shows, it's simply not real.

This is the repetitious pattern of life, sometimes I know what's real, and sometimes I blend into the chaotic patterns of the day. But I seize this moment as an opportunity for change and growth because I know how much I miss when I take on the frenzy.

I miss out on feeling joy and giving to the world in a positive way (and it sure needs our love right now). To smile at people who need a smile, to allow someone to merge into traffic, to tell my husband how much I appreciate him, to hug and listen to my daughters instead of being annoyed with them.

So let me try this again. It's 6:00 p.m. and I have the gift of time. I choose my heart over my mind. I choose to practice what I preach. I choose to give the world what it needs. I take a deep breath, and I choose peace.

When Enough is Enough

Saying yes to all of my children's requests or buying them everything they desire is not realistic, nor is it healthy for our relationship.

Too many things and too much yes will lead to wanting more, and the truth is, my daughters are searching for the no. They need someone to set the boundary so they feel intrinsically safe and protected in this limitless world.

❧

We go to Target to buy shoes, but my daughter wants sunglasses, too. When it's time to go to bed she gets frustrated because she wants to keep playing outside. When we are driving in the car she gets upset if we don't listen to her music.

I acknowledge her desires, but I don't always fulfill them. Sometimes she says, "I never get what I want," and I listen because I know she is communicating her feelings, but I know in my heart it isn't true. At some point I have to say, "Enough," because part of my job is deciding when enough is enough.

As parents we tend to feel guilty if we don't fulfill our kids needs, especially if the kids cry or get angry, or if we are trying to make up for something we feel we are not doing. Saying no can be hard for me, too;

I am not immune to guilt. But I also know that my child cannot make me feel guilty; it's something I have to choose to feel.

My daughter's desires are developmentally appropriate; I don't think she is greedy or trying to manipulate me. She is simply being a little girl and asking for what she wants. I respect her ability to ask, but she doesn't always get what she asks for. It can be difficult for her to hear "no" and "enough," but that doesn't mean I won't say it.

I spend time with my daughter every day, I listen to her when she needs to talk, I look her in the eye so she knows I am listening, and I validate her feelings and acknowledge her desires. I hug her, love her, and take care of her.

And at some point I say "enough," for her benefit and for mine. I say "no," because she needs boundaries, they create structure and unbeknownst to her, they provide a sense of safety. And I say "no" so I don't end up resenting her needs. I won't allow her young desires to put a strain on our relationship.

I have learned that all things come and go, so I know her neediness is a phase and that *this too shall pass*. I have no desire to make her feel guilty for her neediness, and I have no desire to carry guilt for not fulfilling her wishes.

Instead, I say "enough" when it has been enough, and I console her if she is upset or angry about my decision. This is how I love and respect my daughter, and this is how I teach her to love and respect herself.

Airport Faith

This experience was an indicator of my personal growth. Years ago this challenge would have put me over the edge, but as I navigated through the busy airport I realized how many new tools I have at my disposal, and how my outlook has shifted from incapable to persevering.

Of course I felt the emotion of the day and questioned the situation, but I never questioned the belief that I would get through it — and be better because of it.

∽

We recently flew to Seattle to visit family. Our plan was to arrive in Seattle, and then my husband would immediately hop another plane to Portland for a work meeting. The girls and I would head to Seattle to visit my friend Nancy. Then around 5:00 p.m. my husband would fly back to Seattle, we would pick him up at the airport, and then head off to see our family.

Sounds good in theory, right? But there were parts we forgot to think through. We had a rental car, but Todd had to pick it up because it was reserved under his name (many calls were made attempting to add my name, but no luck). Once Todd was on his flight to Portland, the girls and

I needed to manage all of the luggage and car seats and find our way to this rental car.

And there were unforeseeable obstacles—a snow storm in Seattle (people were literally ditching their cars on the side of the road because of the snow), a late arrival, and a stroller stuck inside of the plane due to a frozen plane door.

When we landed, Todd bolted off the plane and ran to pick up the rental car, park it, and hopefully make it back through security in time to catch his flight to Portland.

So the girls and I sat and waited for the frozen plane door to become unfrozen (as a Midwestern girl this was hard to understand . . . just throw some hot water on it or something!).

The girls were already tired and cranky from our 5:00 a.m. wake up and four-and-a-half-hour flight, and I was lost in thought, trying to figure out how to manage the remainder of this travel.

As I spaced out, a familiar face walked toward me. We made eye contact and with relief and happiness I said, "Oh, hi there!" My mind was searching for the man's name, but I was just so happy to see somebody I knew. He said nothing and gave me a confused look, and I quickly realized it was Jim Halpert—I mean, John Krasinski.

While I knew everything about his life at *The Office*, he, of course, had no idea who I was.

My embarrassment quickly subsided because the stroller was finally dislodged from the frozen door, so the girls and I ran through the terminal to meet Todd at his Portland gate so we could get the keys to the rental car.

He handed me the keys, quickly explained where it was parked, and uncomfortably mentioned that the roads were snowy and bad and that there was no windshield wiper fluid. He added something about wiping the windows with baby wipes or stopping at a gas station, but I was back in my head, wondering how I would ever get from here to there intact.

So he boarded his plane, I took a deep breath, and it began—time to get through the airport with three children and head down to baggage claim.

We followed the crowd to a busy train, maneuvered our way to baggage claim, and I searched for our baggage claim tickets because the luggage was already packed away somewhere—it had been an hour since the plane actually arrived.

The helpful lady brought out our endless amount of luggage, and she gave me a puzzled look, as if she doubted that we could actually manage this much. I gave her a smile and a thumbs up, but in reality, I completely agreed with her.

In my mind this seemed logistically impossible, something I would have said no to if Todd and I had talked it through in Chicago. But here I was, and it was time to pull from a different place—so I reached deep for humor and faith, my two favorite motivators.

I told the girls that this was an adventure and that we were on a mission to get to the car. My seven-year-old was in charge of the big suitcase, my six-year-old the other suitcase, and I stacked everything else on the stroller with my three-year-old sitting with bags on her lap.

I casually mentioned that yes, this situation stinks, but hey, we would make it, no matter what! Woo hoo!

But first, where were we going? How could we get out of there, where was parking, where was this rental car that we had never seen before? By following another crowd we made our way onto another elevator (dropping and picking up things as we went).

I felt like crying, but I started laughing and talking to myself, and the girls looked at each other like I was nuts.

Then the big obstacle appeared—a long and pushy line for the elevators to the parking garage. If you didn't move fast, you didn't get in, and we were barely moving with all those bags, let alone moving fast.

I started singing to myself, trying to motivate, trying to keep it together. I told the girls this was a test to find our superpower (I spoke to them, but really I was talking to me).

We missed several elevators. Nobody seemed to be paying attention to the singing mother with three girls and an immense amount of luggage, until a large man shooed people out of the way, held open the elevator door, and said, "Come on!"

He was alone, no luggage, and he was wearing a Bears sweatshirt (normal in Chicago, but in Seattle?). I said thank you, he said nothing–he just focused on his Blackberry.

We arrived on our floor and he held open the door, pushed our luggage out, and disappeared behind the closing elevator doors. Obviously amazing, obviously an angel, but I didn't have time or energy to contemplate the immensity of this occurrence.

So, we were off to search for the car, winding in and out of rows, picking up luggage that fell off the stroller, taking breaks to catch our breath, asking random people for directions, trying to stay warm in the 19-degree weather, staying safely distant from passing cars, trying to keep it together. And then twenty minutes later, there it was–the car.

The key worked, the car started, we got everything in, and the girls were buckled.

As I wiped the dirty, fluid-less windows with baby wipes, my three-year-old started sobbing. She let it all go–the stress of the day, the effort, the adventure, and the challenge. The girls and I said nothing, we knew it was a good release; she was doing it for all of us.

Even with the crying, I drove out onto the wet and messy expressway in Seattle with a smile on my face.

The roads were snowy and unplowed, but I was a confident, experienced Chicago driver, and I had completed a daunting task. I had a new reality of what I could do.

I have no desire to experience an airport situation like that again, but I know I have the ability to handle more than I give myself credit for.

Too much thinking and planning is my greatest limitation–it usually offers a yes or a no, but faith and humor offer a, "Why not? Bring it!"

My real work in life is rolling with it, trusting that it will all work out, in airports and otherwise.

And in my heart I know that what I need is always available. Even when my head begs to differ.

Power Struggles

Old belief systems run deep, and sometimes an old message hits us over the head when we least expect it. But it's also an opportunity for awareness—to realize it's simply another opportunity for growth, another step toward our true selves.

～

It's time to go. I walk out the door and head toward my car. But right before I get there I slip on the ice and fall down. Hard.

I swear a few times and then head in the house. I lie flat on my back and breathe.

I know why I fell. A part of myself is protesting my decision.

I am heading to Detroit to surprise my friend Lara for her fortieth birthday. I am only staying one night, but it's still ten hours of driving and a night away from home.

I have Christmas cards to write, presents to wrap, work to do, and of course, three children and a husband that will have to do without me.

But I want to go. This is a decision I made two weeks ago with no hesitation. It came to me in the shower (this is when most of my ideas come, so I tend to take long showers), and I e-mailed Lara's husband immediately to make the plan.

My heart was speaking, but my heart is not the only part of me that has a voice. I have another voice that is practical, planned, and controlled.

This is the part of me that wrote college papers a week before they were due, and the part that enjoys checking tasks off my to-do list. It's the part that meets work deadlines and makes sure that my children get to school on time.

It's an important part of who I am—it's dependable and responsible and I honor what it provides.

But rationale and responsibility can't always be in charge. Constantly living from this place is too stifling, too demanding, and basically not fun, especially because it's afraid to fail. It serves me, but when it has too much power I get stuck.

My heart decisions are free and exciting, fun and inspiring. Like when I decided to change my major to education my junior year in college, and when I moved to Chicago seventeen years ago with no job and no plan.

Or the time that Lara and I decided to fly to Mardi Gras for just twenty-four hours, or when I decided to become a yoga teacher. These were heart decisions—they felt right, but they didn't make sense logically.

So one voice reminds me to keep my feet on the ground and the other voice reminds me to let my spirit to soar. Much of the time they are wonderful partners, but like most partners, they tend to have power struggles.

I take one more deep breath, stand up, and then look in the mirror. I say out loud to my practical self: "It's a good choice to go to Detroit today, so let's go." I get in my car, turn on my new CD and drive off.

And I don't even need my GPS—I already know I'm headed in the right direction.

Let's Be Clear—What Do We Really Want for Our Children?

I don't know how to fix the educational system in our country. I don't have the information or knowledge to tackle such a huge issue, but I know for sure that the problem is not just in the schools. The values of our culture, society, and families play an undisputable role in the rise or fall of our academic institutions, and more important, the overall welfare of our children.

∽

When I ask parents what they really want for their children, the most common response is: "I just want my kids to be happy." This is great in concept, but what does it really mean?

Be honest—what does happiness really mean to you? Do you want your children to work super hard so they are the smartest in class? Do you want them to constantly practice their sport so they are the best athlete? Do you want your children to have the best grades and test scores so they can go to the best university? Do you want your children to be powerful, rich, and famous?

I think we have confused happiness with overachieving, competition, and being the best. These concepts are no longer in balance in our culture;

they have become the norm rather than the extreme. We are quickly losing sight of what kids really need to live full and meaningful lives.

And the crazy thing is that it's pretty simple—kids just need to be kids. They need time and space to play, dream, and be creative. Not just in an art class where teachers are telling them what to do or make, but open-ended time and space to be messy, dirty, crazy creative.

They also need downtime so they can dive into their imagination (the best imaginative play is often preceded by boredom). Children need to be silly, loud, and expansive, and they need time away from television and structured activities so they are free to tap into their own vision, thoughts, and dreams.

Yes, children need to learn how to read, write, and do math, but this kind of intelligence will come with time and practice. With educational and parental support they will get it—it may not be in exact alignment with the school's schedule, or it may be at a different pace than their older sister or the kid they sit next to, but they will get it.

More important, we need to focus on our children's emotional intelligence—they need to know how to be with people, how to take responsibility, how to compromise, how to handle challenging situations, and how to give back to a community.

As my girls get older I couldn't care less if they are the smartest ones in their classroom. I just want them to be comfortable in the classroom. I want them to enjoy learning, I want them to enjoy their friendships, and I want them to discover tools to deal with challenging academic or social experiences.

I want them to value knowledge and stay curious. I want them to work with partners and groups so they know how to work in a team. I want them to trust their instincts and understand that there are many definitions of the word "smart."

After screening "Race to Nowhere" the other night, I found myself very emotional, almost in pain about what was reflected in this documentary. My hopes and dreams for my children's education are at risk in a system that is solely focused on test scores and overachieving.

The movie showed wonderful teachers leaving the profession because they were expected to only teach to a test, and it shared stories of children whose stress levels were so high they wanted to leave school altogether, harm themselves physically with drugs or sleep deprivation, or, even worse, take their own lives.

Why do they want to do this? Because of one test, one class, one grade, or one non-acceptance letter into a premier university.

I loved college–I highly recommend the experience–but not so much that I would let my children harm themselves to get in, staying up all night to study, taking other people's pills to stay focused, or completely losing themselves so they can please others. This is not my definition of success.

I expect my children to go to school, do their best and ask for help when they need it.

I also expect my children to play, have a hobby, go to the park, and eat dinner with the family. I know for sure they are not a test score or a grade; that is just one very small piece of their bigger self. I can guarantee that class rank will not dictate their future happiness.

Some of my favorite people in the world were not the best students. Their grades were fair, but their lives were full–they were social, musical, creative, and funny.

Some went to college, some didn't go right away, and some didn't go at all, but almost all of them eventually found meaningful relationships and fulfilling professions. They are still great people to be around; they are still full of life, just like when they were young.

My grades were pretty good, but I was an awful test-taker. When I took the PSAT my high school guidance counselor told me that my score was "unacceptable" and that I would be unable to handle college coursework. Based on one test, a moment in time, he was determining my educational fate.

This one person's opinion could have dictated my life's path if I hadn't had parents that begged to differ.

I'm almost forty years old and I am still a poor test-taker (too much gray, people . . . it's hard for me to find one right answer), but I have pursued numerous degrees and certifications and I can't remember a time that I haven't been in school. I am in love with learning and I feel free to do what I love.

I know people who were exceptional test-takers who went to the best universities and found high-paying/high-status jobs, but many of them are doing work they dislike. They feel trapped by their obligation, the money, the amount of time and effort they put into getting where they are now.

They feel disconnected from their families and disconnected from themselves. They talk to me about finding their passion; they talk to me about getting back to what makes them feel good. Perfect grades, the right university, and a high paying job are not the essential pathways to a happy life.

As parents we have to wake up and realize when we are defining our children based on their achievements, rather than who they are. We have to realize when we are praising them for performing rather than for being good people.

We need to become conscious of what we really want for our children. Is our affection and pride only reserved for academic and extracurricular achievement? Or can we begin to see the value in their hobbies, their relationships, and their ability to know and love themselves?

It's difficult to do this when family, friends, neighbors, and institutions say differently. It's difficult to see what is important when we are bombarded with images that tell us that fame, money and power are the only worthy achievements.

But we know better, so it's time to live and teach what we know. These are our children, the people we love the most, so we need to share the truth.

Educational pursuits are valuable, important, and necessary in our culture, but formal education isn't enough.

We need our children to understand the importance of self-respect, compassion, and creativity. We need to teach them that true happiness is not about a score, a grade, an award, or a job; it's about connection to self, connection to others, and connection to this world we share.

Touching Shoulders

It starts with us. We learn to understand ourselves and love ourselves so we have the energy and empathy to care for our family. As we care for ourselves and our family, our hearts open—we realize the importance of taking care of all people, because we are all one family on this earth. We are all connected, in ways that we realize and in ways that we can't fully understand. It's time to become conscious and see this connection. It's time to care.

❧

Last Friday I got off the train in Chicago and headed to the corner of Madison and Canal. The corner was swamped with people. I found a place to stand as I waited for my husband to pick me up.

I noticed a tall unkempt man walking toward me and I knew immediately he would ask me for money.

As a Chicagoan I am used to being asked for money; it's part of big-city living. I usually give a quick dollar, some change, maybe leftover food or a bottle of water.

But still, I felt some annoyance and discomfort as he approached. *Why is he choosing me in this big crowd of people?* He started his sales pitch, but I was already in my purse, searching for a few dollars.

He reached for the money, looked me in the eye and quietly said, "You know I don't want to ask for anything; you know I don't like doing this."

I held his gaze and realized his vulnerability—he almost sounded like a child. His nose was running and he looked so cold. He reminded me of my children when they need my help. He reminded me of myself when I am scared.

He needed money, but he was asking for something more—validation, understanding, and compassion for his situation.

Maybe he made some poor choices along the way, maybe he was a victim of circumstance, but regardless, he just wanted to be seen. He wanted to be recognized and looked in the eye.

I put my hand over his hand and said, "I know you don't want to do this, I know that." He said, "I want to pay this back, but if I don't see you again, I will give to somebody in your honor." I said, "That would be great, please do that."

He said, "God Bless you." I said it back. And he walked away. I took a deep breath and the thoughts began to flow.

My mission as a parent educator is to help parents see their children. To help parents validate and acknowledge whom their children came here to be. To teach children that they belong and they have a place in this world.

But does it stop there? Children grow into adults and this kind of reassurance is still necessary—people need to know they matter, that they belong, that they are understood.

They need to know they are not alone and that someone is willing to listen. It's important to give this to our families, but it's also important to offer this to our community, our city, our world. This connects us; this is what humanity means.

So today I am writing about this experience at my local coffee shop and an elderly gentleman is sitting nearby, trying to engage me in conversation.

My first response is agitation (*This is work time, I must complete this article!*), but the article I'm writing is the story of the Chicago man.

I am writing about the experience, but did I integrate the lesson? I am sharing so I can teach, but am I practicing what I preach? I decide to push the computer aside so I can really listen and respond to this man.

We talk about the Final Four (he shares his picks), but conversation quickly turns to his life. He is eighty-five (actually he says, "I am fifty-eight, but backwards.") and his wife passed away five years ago.

He says she was beautiful. He says he misses her. He says she loved poetry and he likes to hand out poems she enjoyed to "spread the love."

He reaches into his bag and hands me a wrinkled piece of paper with a photocopied poem. He says it's a special one just for me.

I am glad that I live, that I battle and strive
For the place that I know I must fill;
I am thankful for sorrows; I'll meet with a grin
What fortune may send, good or ill
I may not have wealth, I may not be great,
But I know I shall always be true,
For I have in my life that courage you gave
When once I touched shoulders with you.
~ Unknown

Conclusion

Life lessons are constant, they cannot be avoided, but it is possible to deal with them in a self-aware way; to view all of our experiences as an opportunity for growth and learning.

Many people live somewhat unconsciously, until there is a crisis, a death in the family, or a devastating illness. The crisis wakes them up, makes them ask the big questions, and inspires them to figure out who they are and why they are here. But when the crisis has passed, they often fall back into the same patterns and the same old routine, and forget why they were searching in the first place.

Being a parent should be our daily wake up call. It's our responsibility to take care of ourselves and be conscious of our choices so we can effectively raise our children. It's our job to teach the next generation self-respect and self-understanding, but it's unfair to ask our children to do what we do not do for ourselves.

It's time to practice some self-love and self-awareness, and the first step is to slow down and listen. Every day for five minutes let go of all the noise around you—the phones, computers, traffic, and voices, and really listen to what the voice in your head says to you. It's often not very nice, and it's scary to realize that this is often the voice that guides you through your day. Know that this voice is only one part of you—it may be hurt, cynical, or afraid. Trust that there are many other parts of you waiting to come out, waiting for an opportunity to be heard.

To find these parts of yourself, take some time to realize what you love and what you don't, what gives you energy and what drains your energy. Choose to spend time with people you enjoy and volunteer or participate in activities you really love. Start taking steps toward being yourself rather than who everyone else expects you to be.

Make yourself a priority instead of putting everybody and everything else first. Martyrdom and suffering may have been taught to you, but you don't have to accept these philosophies as truth. It's time to examine these beliefs, to realize that you have the right to be aware, enjoy life, and find contentment.

And from contentment comes the realization that you are not perfect, and you never will be. You have challenges and concerns and you make mistakes. You have uncomfortable emotions and you don't always make the right choices. These are inevitable parts of life, and realizing this will allow you to let go of shame and guilt.

Instead of reliving your mistakes and self-sabotaging you will learn how to forgive your past and move forward. Heal what needs to be healed by feeling what needs to felt and ask for help when you need it. Make a decision to confront what needs to be dealt with rather than avoid what is. Understand that your children will have challenging experiences, too, and they will learn their coping tools by watching you.

Understand that your children's perspective on life is dictated by how they feel inside. They need to know that they are enough and that they have tools to deal with whatever comes their way. They need to know that if they feel stuck or scared that you are willing to listen with love and trust rather than fear and judgment. Stop talking so much and start listening to what they have to say—notice that they already have so much information and internal guidance. Notice their natural wisdom and their innate creativity. Help them hold on to these gifts instead of telling them to be like everybody else.

Children just want to be heard, understood, and validated. This may sound simple, but if you are overwhelmed, unconscious, or drowning in your own challenges you will not have the space to fully support their needs. Take care of yourself so you have room and patience to be present for these relationships, and be aware and open-minded so you can really hear your children's perspective. They are wise, and they have ideas and information to share. If you recognize this, your children's sense of worth will be validated and they will inherently understand that they have a voice in the world.

Realize that you have a voice in the world, too. Stay focused on your dreams, keep learning, and trust that anything is possible. Be aware of your feelings, ask for help when you need it, and understand your importance. You have gifts to share with the world and you are a role model for a future generation. Enjoy your life and pass it on.

13533102R00051

Made in the USA
Lexington, KY
05 February 2012